PASSION TRACKER

The Beginners 7 Steps To Unleash Your True Passion

And Make It Your Profession

GLADYS GLOBAL

COPYRIGHT © 2020

Any rights retained. Without the prior written permission of the author, no portion of this publication can be copied, circulated or transmitted in any medium or through any means, including photocopying, documenting or other electronic or mechanical methods, except for brief excerpts contained in critical reviews and some other non-commercial uses allowed under copyright law.

TABLE OF CONTENTS

Introduction..1

Discover Your Passion..3

How Do I Find My Purpose And Live It..........................5

Your Passion and Purpose: What You Should Know...................8

7 Steps On How to Identify and Clarify Your Purpose in Life...14

8 Reasons Why You Need Clear Vision 19

How to Activate the Power Within..22

Finding the Power Within You to Succeed in Life And Business..25

INTRODUCTION

When you look back on your life, will it be with disappointment, or will it be with great joy of a life lived to the full extent of your potential?

You are the only one that can decide to embark on your true-life journey to discover your true purpose. Many people believe and fall victim to life's biggest lie that life is out of control and working against them.

When you are inspired by a passion or purpose which lights up your life, your world expands beyond bounds and previously conceived boundaries, and you discover yourself to be a greater person than you can imagine.

How do we find our Destiny (Destination)? Everything in life has a purpose - be it a pet, a tree, a flower, and every living person.

Passions are the keys to your destiny - they lead you to discover who you are and what you are here to do in this life. What are your gifts, and what are you to do with them? When you align with these, you begin to live a renewed life with boundless energy. You will be amazed as you start to attract the things you need in your life.

- Your Passion - is the gifts you have or the things you love doing.
- Your Purpose - as you focus on your passion, your purpose (opportunities to use your gifts) will emerge.

Find and do the things you are passionate about, and you will never have to work another day in your life. What you do will be pure joy - more like a hobby or holiday than going to work.

DISCOVER YOUR PASSION

Look inside yourself and find the things that make you truly happy - yes, we all have them - look again, they are there. As they emerge, write them down and keep them where you will be regularly reminded.

Spend a few minutes each day reflecting on your passions, and you'll soon see opportunities dropping into your mind and your life as to how you can begin to develop your gifts and how you can use them in service to others.

Along your path of discovery, there will be those that will endeavor to discourage you. Do not let anyone steal them from you - do not be distracted. It is only by persevering that you will achieve and live out your passion and purpose.

Be patient in perseverance if your passions don't emerge. Give yourself time and permission to explore this more deeply. Be kind to yourself as you embark on this journey. Reward yourself for early steps and achievements. It is a journey of realization which can take some while.

Sometimes we bury our passions deeply because of something that has happened in our life or out of the fear of what may be asked of us should we open this area of our life. We cannot open ourselves to our passion or our purpose until we are prepared to go beyond our comfort zone, scary perhaps, rewarding definitely.

HOW DO I FIND MY PURPOSE AND LIVE IT

As human beings, we have an instinctive drive to evolve, improve, and innovate to make things faster, smarter, easier, better, and more sustainable. With technology, we are exponentially expanding the scope of what is possible. But even as new opportunities arise, many people find their old jobs obsolete or changing, and their skill sets ready for an overhaul. Now, more than ever, it is essential to be clear about what is most important to you and how you choose to express your purpose through your life's work.

Many people identify with their occupation. One of the most common questions, when people meet for the first time, is: "What do you do?" So as careers shift, it can influence self-perception. Work is a way to live your purpose and contribute to society.

When a seemingly solid foundation of a career shift, it can often lead to serious self-reflection or even a temporary feeling of loss. It is wise to begin asking timeless questions about your purpose and your mission: What is my purpose? Why am I here? How will I fulfill my destiny?

When you find your purpose, your livelihood and sense of self aren't tied to a particular job or position. This is freedom: when your thoughts, words, and actions are aligned with your purpose, and you live from a space of inner harmony. Knowing the most appropriate opportunities will reveal themselves.

You will find your purpose when you make conscious choices based on what is essential - not what is necessary or required, but what is of your essence: who you are and who you choose to be. You access this wisdom through stillness.

Stillness is where you source the insight to know yourself, love your life, and live your purpose. Your intuitive wisdom grows, and your purpose becomes clear as you honor, welcome, and allow stillness to be the nucleus of every thought, word, and deed.

You can also find your purpose by paying attention to what you love doing? What are you really good at? Where do you slip into timelessness? What is a natural action for you? If you could give anything to people, what would it be? The things which bring you joy are clues to your purpose.

Lastly, education and self-development are also important in finding your purpose.

YOUR PASSION AND PURPOSE: WHAT YOU SHOULD KNOW

Why am I here? What is my purpose? Those are tough questions. They defy simple answers. They open up other, even trickier questions. They tap at the door of religion, toy with the ideas of philosophers, and often leave us completely dumbfounded, even after a great deal of thinking.

Finding our purposes is essential, though. It's a necessary step to genuine happiness and a life that feels meaningful. When you don't know your purpose, it's hard to move in the right direction and far too easy to get lost in things about which you don't care.

So, how can you find your purpose? Here are a few things you can do to move toward that vital part of building the wonderful life you deserve.

First, think about what you love. Consider your deepest, strongest passions. What makes you feel whole? What excites you? Your purpose will always serve that passion. Your purpose in life is to use that passion as fuel as you move toward personal growth and achievement.

Second, remember those times in your life when everything felt right. For some, those may be extended periods. Others may have only experience fleeting moments. All of us have had that remarkable sense that we were doing the right thing at some point. Consider those times and look for clues and common traits that might reveal your purpose.

Third, commit to being honest with yourself. Don't try to impose the purposes others have chosen on your life. You must answer to yourself and find meaning in your life that belongs uniquely to you. Your opinion is the one that matters here. Deal with it honestly.

Some people discover their purpose in life early and almost effortlessly. Some of us need to work harder to reveal what will put the wind in our sails. By isolating your passions, reflecting on your past, and being wholly honest with yourself, you can find your purpose, opening the door to the remarkable life you so richly deserve.

So, to thrive and prosper in a changing world while creating life's work that expresses your purpose and passion, here are a few suggestions:

1. Know Thyself

Sincerely ask the question, "Who am I?" Who are you at your core? What is most important to you in life? What is essential? Throughout your life, what have been the innate elements that inspire and drive you - beyond jobs, beliefs, relationships, the past, or any stories or identities that you may have had? Who are you in your essence? What makes you unique? What ignites your passion? In what way do you reveal your gifts? Your purpose will emanate from your sense of self. It resides within you.

_____
_____
_____
_____
_____
_____
_____
_____
_____
_____

2. Recognize Your Purpose

Your purpose is your unique offering. It is your reason for being. It is the source fueling your vision. Your purpose answers the question, "Why am I here?" It is your North Star - the bright light, which guides and directs you as you adventure through life. When you make conscious choices grounded in your essence, you reveal and refine your purpose.

Ask yourself, "What do I stand for at my best?" Ask, "What is my unique contribution to the world?" Look to your past for clues: if you string together the defining moments of your life, they will often point to a theme or a definite calling.

_____
_____
_____
_____
_____
_____
_____
_____

3. Live Your Mission

Your mission is your purpose in action. It is how you express your purpose through what you do. You live your mission by expressing your essence consistently through the choices you make. Through your mission, you answer the question, "How may I serve?" How will you create the life you envision? How will your creations inspire others and enrich the world around you? What will you give? When you live your mission, you consciously direct the course of change.

_____
_____
_____
_____
_____
_____
_____
_____
_____
_____
_____
_____

7 STEPS ON HOW TO IDENTIFY AND CLARIFY YOUR PURPOSE IN LIFE

There are two parts to realizing your purpose in life. The first part is your general-purpose, which is simply how you want to be remembered at the end of your life. The second part of discovering your purpose is figuring out how you intend to carry out your general-purpose through your specific talents, skills, and abilities.

1. Take a Personal Retreat From Your Daily Routine

Finding your life purpose is perhaps the single most important answer you will have to discover for yourself, and it stands to reason that in order to find your purpose, you will need to dedicate 100% of your mental and spiritual energy towards that effort. With all the chaos surrounding our daily lives, it's not practical to even attempt to find your life's purpose while managing the other responsibilities of your life.

2. Identify Your Core Competencies

Make a list of eight things that you are really good at doing. These can include specific talents, skills, and abilities that you have. Don't worry about your purpose at this point. Just list your best skills. My core competencies include writing, coaching, and teaching.

3. Identify Your Passions

Make a list of four things that you are passionate about and love doing. These are things that you would gladly do without pay because they are a constant source of joy and happiness for you. Your list of passions will most likely be a duplicate of your list of core competencies because you usually do well what you are also passionate about.

4. Identify Your Legacy

Your legacy is how you would like to be remembered after you are gone from this world. If you had your chapter in a history book, what would be written about your life? What contributions would you have made to society? Brainstorm on a legacy by writing eight ideas and then use a tournament-style draw system to prioritize your list down to the most important legacy.

5. Link your passions with your purpose

Remember that having a general-purpose is not enough to make it meaningful. You must also decide on the method that you will use to achieve that purpose. Our purpose might be to help other people, but our plans for achieving that purpose might be very different.

6. Create a Purpose Statement

Your personal statement of purpose is a concise declaration of why you are here in this world. It's made up of two parts: a general-purpose and a method. Keep your purpose statement as concise as possible and limited to only two sentences. Your first sentence is what you intend to do with your life--the legacy you came up with in step 3. My personal statement of purpose has always been to put a smile on people's faces as I serve to make their dreams come true.

7. How to Inspire a Clear Vision for Your Business

Let's get a couple of definitions out of the way first:

- **Vision** - the big picture dream about your business
- **Purpose** - why you exist
- **Mission** - the task you set out to achieve

- **Goal** - what you will do to accomplish that task

Creating a clear vision for your business takes some thought, big thought, because this is the one time where you can think larger than you normally would, and the opportunity to think in terms of what you hope to see if you accomplished all your related objectives ultimately.

Next is why you are the one to fulfill the vision and then how you will go about it, ending with a stated goal. The goal statement itself should be big, and all-encompassing followed with many smaller goals and objectives that relate to each strategy.

These four components should guide and direct your ultimate business and marketing plan. Each of your statements should be clear, compelling, and concise.

The vision is the thing that keeps you up at night dreaming and imagining. Purpose is what wakes you up in the morning, and mission is your focus. Therefore, the way in which you inspire a clear vision for your business is to develop one. Dream big!

The way you make it clear is by telling everyone in your business, on your team, and your clients that this is your vision. Then, of course, back it up with a solid business plan, consistent action, and follow-through. It is then, and only then, it becomes part of everyone's reality and not just your own.

8 REASONS WHY YOU NEED CLEAR VISION

Having a clear vision is like a dial on a radio station. I'm sure we all have a favorite radio station. But what if you are tuned into 95.5 when your favorite station is 95.7? Yes, you may still hear the music, but it's not very clear. What can you do to have that clarity? You need to make a little tweak! Setting yourself to the right station allows yourself to 'see,' 'feel,' 'hear,' and 'taste' your vision!

Also, your clearly written vision will help to alleviate the doubt and willy-nilly misdirection that can occur in any business that lacks a vision.

When you focus with clear intention on what your goals are, you can attract them with little effort. You actually pull things to you instead of chasing after it.

Here are 8 reasons why you need a clear vision to startup that business:

1. Gain insights into why you want something that will help strengthen the vision. Do you want more time to spend traveling or need to experience more joy in your life?
2. Having the vision to see what your future holds ahead gives you inspiration, hope, and motivation to change.
3. The time to reach your goal will be shorter because it's crystal clear on what you want.
4. If you don't have a clue as to what you want, how will you know you have succeeded? You need something as a target, so you know how to measure the results. No vision equals confusion and a lack of motivation.
5. It creates a plan that can be broken down into step by step instructions to take action.
6. The law of attraction and action will assist you in getting life to introduce you to the right people or the right things at the right time. Stay open and aware of opportunities that present themselves to you.
7. It inspires you to get up each morning with renewed enthusiasm to go out and get it.
8. Having a clear vision can force you to think creatively, so you set out to achieve your goal.

PASSION TRACKER 1

No matter who you are, when you gain a clear vision of what you want, you can achieve great things. Reach beyond your limitations and find a vision to see your future.

HOW TO ACTIVATE THE POWER WITHIN

We all have a subconscious mind that can be influenced by new thought patterns, and what we need to focus on is what we hope to achieve in our lifetime.

If our focus is on lack of money, then that is precisely what we'll get. We already have the mental tools necessary to create the scenario we want, but sometimes we need to be shown how to use them.

Remove the lid to your mind with respect to how much you earn and understand that the wealth you are seeking is already there waiting for you. All you have to do is tap into it and discover the power within.

Start picturing yourself in possession of great wealth and then visualize how you're going to spend it. Your subconscious mind cannot tell the difference between you doing something or visualizing yourself doing it.

You cannot have something physically until you have it mentally. Once you achieve this, then you are on your way to developing a prosperity consciousness.

So, how do we activate the power within? Every great man of exploits ever celebrated, was a man who had been able to reach down within to tap into the power within. I know it because the word of God is very clear about it.

Activating the power of God within us involves three steps; it involves you taking a journey of self-evaluation in the light of the word of God. To be able to understand how to activate the power within, you need the word as your manual.

Let me remind you of God's word in Ephesians 3:20 it reads thus: Now unto him, that is able to do exceeding abundantly above all that we ask or think, according to the power that worketh in us, the three steps are hidden in this one verse, when clearly understood can make all the difference in your life.

Also, the power of activation lies within you, my friend. Do you know your thoughts are unspoken words? Therefore, to activate God's power within you, fill your thought dimension with the word of God. For instance, take a look at Phil 4:13 it reads thus: I can do all things through Christ which strengtheneth me, fill your spirit with the ... I can do all things thinking.

Lastly, the power of God will be ignited inside of you as you allow these power thoughts to dominate your spirit. I recommend you walk with my "**40 Words for 40 Days Spiritual and Soul Fitness**" program to ignite the power within you using those words.

FINDING THE POWER WITHIN YOU TO SUCCEED IN LIFE AND BUSINESS

There is only one key to success -- you. The power within you to create the life you want is very real and accessible to everyone. It's as easy as using your mind. There's a reason people say to succeed; you only need to "put your mind to it." With the power of your mind, you can accomplish almost anything. Using it in combination with your senses increases its effectiveness. With vision, you can imagine. With a touch, you can create storyboards of your dreams coming true. And with speech, you can tell yourself all things are possible.

Here are a few simple ways to put the power of your mind to work.

1. Affirmations and Positive Self-Talk

Most people can talk themselves into being sick; the more you say you feel ill, the worse you feel. The same is true in the positive. Say beautiful things and nice things will happen.

Daily affirmations and regular use of positive self-talk will, over time, put you in the mindset to create accept the success that you experience.

2. The Sticky-Note Trick

Many people have a hard time remembering their affirmations. It is also easy to forget to recite them daily. Write each one on a large notecard-sized sticky and post them in places you see every day. On your bathroom mirror. Next to the kitchen light switch. Recite them each time you see them.

3. Using Imagery and Meditation

The power of your imagination is unending. Spending time each day in meditation will eliminate the clutter of your mind and allow crystal clear direction to enter. Visualize success by vividly imagining it, and you will intuitively bring into your life the people and situations you need to bring it to fruition.

The power within your mind is an amazing thing. Used properly, it can yield astonishing results. Combine your thought process with any of the five senses, and you've created a new tool for success. The only secret to success is within yourself, within your power, and well within your reach.

The bottom line here is that you have Power Within, and you can access it. It is okay to wonder about if you can, but you must take steps to try and access it more and more. As you get better at it, you will create a habit of it, and then it will come as a natural response, every time you need it.

We all have this power inside of us, and we simply have to find the tools to access and use it to our benefit. We all can do it; we just have to know how.

49-DAY PASSION TRACKER WORKSHOP SHEET

They say, "Failing to plan is planning to fail". So plan!

P.E = Physical Exercise 45 minutes minimum every day.

Goal = The projects/business/gift/talent/passion that you're working towards to make it a reality. 45 minutes minimum every day.

PASSION TRACKER 1

	MONDAY	TUESDAY	WEDNESDAY	THURSDAY	FRIDAY	SATURDAY	SUNDAY	OBSERVATIONS
TRIAL WEEK	1. PE 45 Mins 2. GOAL 45 m							
WEEK 1								
WEEK 2								
WEEK 3								
WEEK 4								
WEEK 5								
WEEK 6								
WEEK 7								

(This is an example of how I design on an A4 paper every time I do the Passion Tracker Challenge). But now I print it off ☺

Passion Tracker

	M	T	W	T	F	S	S
TRIAL WEEK							
WEEK 1							
WEEK 2							
WEEK 3							
WEEK 4							
WEEK 5							
WEEK 6							
WEEK 7							

Passion Tracker

	M	T	W	T	F	S	S
TRIAL WEEK							
WEEK 1							
WEEK 2							
WEEK 3							
WEEK 4							
WEEK 5							
WEEK 6							
WEEK 7							

Passion Tracker

	M	T	W	T	F	S	S
TRIAL WEEK							
WEEK 1							
WEEK 2							
WEEK 3							
WEEK 4							
WEEK 5							
WEEK 6							
WEEK 7							

Passion Tracker

	M	T	W	T	F	S	S
TRIAL WEEK							
WEEK 1							
WEEK 2							
WEEK 3							
WEEK 4							
WEEK 5							
WEEK 6							
WEEK 7							

Passion Tracker

	M	T	W	T	F	S	S
TRIAL WEEK							
WEEK 1							
WEEK 2							
WEEK 3							
WEEK 4							
WEEK 5							
WEEK 6							
WEEK 7							

PASSION TRACKER 1

Passion Tracker

	M	T	W	T	F	S	S
TRIAL WEEK							
WEEK 1							
WEEK 2							
WEEK 3							
WEEK 4							
WEEK 5							
WEEK 6							
WEEK 7							

Passion Tracker

	M	T	W	T	F	S	S
TRIAL WEEK							
WEEK 1							
WEEK 2							
WEEK 3							
WEEK 4							
WEEK 5							
WEEK 6							
WEEK 7							

www.ingramcontent.com/pod-product-compliance
Lightning Source LLC
Chambersburg PA
CBHW050321220526
45465CB00005B/2075